T'ANG DYNASTY POEMS

translated by

JOHN KNOEPFLE
AND
WANG SHOUYI

SPOON RIVER POETRY PRESS

1985

This book is printed in part with funds provided by the Illinois Arts Council, a state organization, and by the National Endowment for the Arts. Our many thanks.

Typesetting by D. J. Graphics, Peoria, Illinois and Paul Brink Associates, Minneapolis, Minnesota.
Printing by M & D Printers, Henry, Illinois.
Cover: detail from Chu Lun-Han, *Landscape*, hanging scroll, ink and light color on paper, 18th century. Robert Allerton Collection of The Art Institute of Chicago. Copyright (C) The Art Institute of Chicago. All rights reserved.

ISBN: 0-933180-76-4 pb
      0-933180-84-5 hb

T'ANG DYNASTY POEMS

a few lines after returning to my hometown

   —he zhizhang

left home a child and came back an old old man
my hair has turned gray but my accent is the same
kids in the village did not know me when we met
said where did the guest come from with the funny smile

回鄉偶書

賀知章

少小離家老大回，
鄉音未改鬢毛衰。
兒童相見不相識，
笑問客從何處來。

climbing the stork kiosk

　　　　—wang zhihuan

the pale sun is sinking behind the mountain
and the yellow river is running into the sea
do you want to look at the end of the earth
which is hundreds of miles away
well you have to climb these steps to do that

登鸛雀樓

　　　　王之渙

白日依山盡，
黃河入海流，
欲窮千里目，
更上一層樓。

liangzhou song

  —wang zhihuan

the yellow river rises in the tall white clouds
a town is isolated there
it is locked in mountains thousands of feet high
no need for the qiang flute
playing "poplar and willow" so sad a song
the spring wind never comes to that place
it never warms the other side of yumen pass

凉州詞

    王之渙

黃河遠上白雲間，
一片孤城萬仞山。
羌笛何須怨楊柳，
春風不度玉門關。

at dawn in spring

　—meng haoran

slept so well I didn't know it was dawn
birds singing in every courtyard woke me up
the wind and rain troubled my dream last night
I think of all those petals swept to the ground

春曉

孟浩然

春眠不覺曉，
處處聞啼鳥。
夜來風雨聲，
花落知多少？

anchored at night on the river in jiande county

　　—meng haoran

my boat lies at anchor
below yandu mountain

it is sundown and I feel even more
the homesickness of the traveler

this is so vast a place
even the nearest trees
seem small on the horizon

now the moon sails in clear water
it seems so near
I could almost touch it

宿建德江

　　　　孟浩然

移舟泊烟渚，
日暮客愁新。
野曠天低樹，
江清月近人。

border duty

—wang changling

qing hai clouds shadow the snow-capped mountains
yumen pass is a long way to the west

and the border town with high battlements
it is beyond the pass

this soldier has fought many times
has defended his barren place

he has met the loulan horsemen in his armor
the gleam of his polished armor

he says if I cannot kill the enemy
I will never go home

從軍行

王昌齡

青海長雲暗雪山，
孤城遙望玉門關。
黃沙百戰穿金甲，
不斬樓蘭終不還。

beyond the border

     —wang changling

the brilliant moon and the pass speak to me
of victories we won in qin and han dynasties

our men hound the invaders
they haven't come home yet

if that high-stepping general
from dragon city were still living

he would command our troops
and no hu horsemen would cross yin mountain

出塞

王昌齡

秦時明月漢時關，
萬里長征人未還。
但使龍城飛將在，
不教胡馬度陰山。

7

bride's complaint

—wang changling

she feels happy in her room this spring morning
puts on her make-up and goes to the balcony

suddenly she sees below her in the garden
poplar and willow in fresh new colors

thinks bitterly how could she have let him go off
looking for a post as a high court official

閨怨

王昌齡

閨中少婦不知愁，
春日凝妝上翠樓；
忽見陌頭楊柳色，
悔教夫婿覓封侯。

the ninth day of the ninth month
in the lunar calendar I think of my brothers
on the north side of the mountain

—wang wei

lonesome as an unexpected guest
in a strange village
I miss my family twice over
whenever we celebrate the good festivals

so far from home I picture
the hills where my brothers ramble
and the sweet-scented cornel
tucked in everyone's jacket but my own

九月九日憶山東兄弟

王維

獨在異鄉爲異客，
每逢佳節倍思親。
遙知兄弟登高處，
遍插茱萸少一人。

wei city song

—wang wei

a dawn rain comes
and settles the dust in wei city

hotels are soaked deep in dark wet colors
but the willows are a brighter green

why not one more drink for the road
although we have had a few already

once you go west of yang pass
old friends are hard to come by

渭城曲

王維

渭城朝雨浥輕塵，
客舍青青柳色新。
勸君更盡一杯酒，
西出陽關無故人。

thoughts on a quiet evening

—li bai

the floor is flooded with moonlight
frost covered the old earth like that

I gaze at the moon
shimmering in a dark hour

sad and homesick
I bow down my head

靜夜思

李白

床前明月光，
疑是地上霜。
舉頭望明月，
低頭思故鄉。

qiupu song

       —li bai

fire booms in the forge
lights up the wide universe

hammer blows shower with sparks
that vanish in purple smoke

I tell you this is a night
for contrast

the red face of the smith
the white face of the moon

the clanging of the hammer
the song of the smith

they shatter the dark cold
down the long valley

秋浦歌

李白

爐火照天地，
紅星亂紫烟。
赧郎明月夜，
歌曲動寒川。

*li bai accompanied his uncle on a visit
to dongting lake and wrote this poem
after getting drunk*

—li bai

boat floating around jun mountain
I will flatten this mountain

make the scenery better
water from xiang river will run easily here

ba ling a small town beside the lake
boat comes to this town
a good place to drink a lot of wine in

my uncle and I
we were three sheets to the wind
that fall day on dongting lake

陪侍郎叔遊洞庭醉後
李白

划却君山好，
平鋪湘水流。
巴陵無限酒，
醉殺洞庭秋。

13

song of the moon on emei mountain

—li bai

autumn and a half moon on emei mountain
shadow of the moon dipped into pingchang river

the current is flowing in the river

I left the port of ching xi this night
and set out for the three gorges of the yangtze
the gorges that narrow the sky overhead

I long for someone I care for
my good companion
but I cannot see him

sailing by yu zhou in the quick night

峨嵋山月歌

李白

峨嵋山月半輪秋，
影入平羌江水流。
夜發清溪向三峽，
思君不見下渝州。

14

watching the lu mountain falls

  —li bai

purple smoke rises from the mountaintop
the peak looks like an incense burner in the sunlight
far away I see the valley stretching before me
the whole waterfall hangs there
the torrent dropping three thousand feet
straight down to the valley floor
I think it must be the milky way
spilling to the earth from the heavens

望廬山瀑布

   李白

日照香爐生紫烟，
遙看瀑布掛前川。
飛流直下三千尺，
疑是銀河落九天。

view of tienmen mountain

  —li bai

I can see the yangtze cut
as my boat reaches tienmen mountain

the green water running east
turns here in a fierce whirl

green ranges of the mountain
rush toward me on both sides of the river

a single sail bends with the wind
where the sun comes up on the water

望天門山

　　　　李白

天門中斷楚江開，
碧水東流至此回。
兩岸青山相對出，
孤帆一片日邊來。

to wang lun

—li bai

I am on board
and the boat ready to sail
when suddenly there is a song
and the rhythm of feet
dancing on the shore

the water in peach flower pond
is a thousand fathoms
but it cannot be deeper
than the affection of wang lun
who comes to wave me goodby

贈汪倫

李白

李白乘舟將欲行，
忽聞岸上踏歌聲。
桃花潭水深千尺，
不及汪倫送我情。

lines while hearing a flute playing
one spring night in luoyang city

—li bai

I don't know whose house it is
the sound of the jade flute comes from
like a secret spirited on the wind
this evening in april

it enters every home
with that song "breaking the willow branches"
and we know what pain
remembering the hometown brings

春夜洛城聞笛
　　　李白

誰家玉笛暗飛聲，
散入春風滿洛城。
此夜曲中聞折柳，
何人不起故園情。

seeing meng haoran off

    —li bai

my old friend leaves yellow crane pavilion
he is going to the west

sailing to yangzhou in march
while blossoms curl like smoke on the river

how far away the lone sail
fading into the clear blue sky

only the yangtze river remains
it is flowing at the edge of the world

黃鶴樓送孟浩然之廣陵
李白

故人西辭黃鶴樓，
烟花三月下楊州。
孤帆遠影碧空盡，
唯見長江天際流。

leaving baidi city in the early morning

—li bai

baidi city on the mountaintop
was still swathed in red clouds
when my boat sailed from the foothills
early that morning

I reached jiangling city in the evening
logging hundreds of miles in one day
monkeys were screaming
on both banks of the yangtze

they never let up the whole day's travel
while our frail boat dashed between
a thousand mountains lining the river

早發白帝城

李白

朝辭白帝彩雲間，
千里江陵一日還。
兩岸猿聲啼不住，
輕舟已過萬重山。

taken in for the night in my host's house
on lotus mountain when I was caught in the snow

—liu changqing

the great dark mountain
seems far away at sundown
this small white cottage
it is a poor place but comfortable
in such cold weather

the dog barks
at the gate of sticks and branches
my host has come home
he has worked long hours
in the wind-driven snow

逢雪宿芙蓉山主人

劉長卿

日暮蒼山遠，
天寒白屋貧。
柴門聞犬吠，
風雪夜歸人。

21

alone and looking for flowers on the river bank

—du fu

flowers applaud both sides of the path
in the courtyard of auntie huang si

blossoms thick as sunshine
hang from the heavy branches

the butterfly will not abandon any flower
he dances from one to the other
only now and then

the oriole at his golden pleasure
sings freely and so beautifully
tra la heigh ho no worries today

江畔獨步尋花

杜甫

黃四娘家花滿蹊，
千朵萬朵壓枝低。
留連戲蝶時時舞，
自在嬌鶯恰恰啼。

song for hua the mighty general

       —du fu

in jin cheng the flutes and the strings
you hear them so loud even in the daytime

the melody fades in the river wind
and half in the towering clouds above us

oh it should never be played here
it belongs to the emperor's heaven

we thank you for what is not ours
but the emperor will be hearing it also

贈花卿

杜甫

錦城絲管日紛紛，
半入江風半入雲。
此曲只應天上有，
人間能得幾回聞？

little poem

—du fu

two yellow orioles sing in the tender green willow
a line of herons crosses the blue sky

when you open the west-facing window
the snow is framed on the summit of the mountain

and the ships that will sail east for dong wu
they lie at anchor in the sun-filled doorway

七言絕句

杜甫

兩個黃鸝鳴翠柳，
一行白鷺上青天。
窗含西嶺千秋雪，
門泊東吳萬里船。

five words to a line poem

—du fu

river green whiter water birds
mountain green red flowers afire
another spring dying in colors
what year sends me homeward

五言絕句

杜甫

江碧鳥逾白，
山青花欲燃。
今春看又過，
何日是歸年？

the eight stone battle formations

    —du fu

he had the magnificence
that overwhelmed the three kingdoms

his eight battle formations
struck everyone with terror and awe

his stones are still in place
despite the flooding of five hundred years

we are left with his shame as he watched
his rash lord turn on the wu allies

八陣圖

　　　　杜甫

功蓋三分國，
名成八陣圖。
江流石不轉，
遺恨失吞吳。

meeting li guinian in the south of the yangtze

     —du fu

I saw you often in king qi's house
your name came up several times
at the receptions of cui the ninth

this is the best season
in the south of the yangtze
the scenery is excellent

but the petals have fallen
it is too late for flowers
and now we see each other again

江南逢李龜年

      杜甫

岐王宅里尋常見，
崔九堂前幾度聞。
正是江南好風景，
落花時節又逢君。

meeting the envoy on his way to the capital

　　　—jin cen

I see that the road is long and endless
when I look back to my hometown in the east
I wipe my eyes on my sleeves
but there are too many tears to dry them

now because we meet on horseback on the highway
there is no place to find a brushpen or paper
so please take this message to my family in the capital
I feel all right and no one has threatened me

逢入京使

　　　岑參

故園東望路漫漫，
雙袖龍鐘淚不乾。
馬上相逢無紙筆，
憑君傳語報平安。

the western ravine in chuzhou

　　　—wei yingwu

I am sad for the tranquil grass
that grows alongside the ravine

orioles are singing above it
hidden in the great trees

spring sends rain to the river
it rushes in a flood in the evening

the little boat tugs at its line
by the ferry landing

here in the wilderness
it responds to the current

there is no one on board

滁州西澗

　　　　韋應物

獨憐幽草澗邊生，
上有黃鸝深樹鳴。
春潮帶雨晚來急，
野渡無人舟自橫。

29

reply to zhang puye's border song

     —lu lun

No. 2

it is getting dark and the woods darker
and the uneasy wind
disturbs the meadow

the commander drew his bowstring
taut in the night

we looked for his feathered shaft
when dawn came again

we found it where he drove it
deep in the pinnacle
that jutted from the rock

和張仆射塞下曲（之二）

盧綸

林暗草驚風，
將軍夜引弓。
平明尋白羽，
沒在石棱中。

30

reply to zhang puye's border song

    —lu lun

No. 3

dark of the moon
and the wild geese flying high

chan yu lost the battle
and fled into the night

our light cavalry
quick mounted and chased him

came back saddle-sore and exhausted
sleet freezing on their bows and knives

和張仆射塞下曲（之三）

盧綸

月黑雁飛高，
單于夜遁逃。
欲將輕騎逐，
大雪滿弓刀。

sentiments in fall

    —lu lun

so many years today
my hair sparse and white

and this is another autumn
leaves yellow and dry

I scratch my head
and complain to these leaves

the deep sadness
they have fallen to share

傷秋

盧綸

歲去人頭白，
秋來樹葉黃。
搔頭向黃葉，
與爾共悲傷。

listening to zheng music

     —li duan

the resonant strings tremble
on the golden pillar of zheng instrument

slender white fingers dance at the frets
there before the bed of general zhou

she touches a wrong note now and then
coaxing a glance from the general

聽箏

李端

鳴箏金粟柱，
素手玉房前。
欲得周郎顧，
時時誤拂絃。

south of the yangtze river song

      —li yi

I got myself married to a merchant
who lives beside qutang lake

he goes off in the morning
and works for his money all night long

the tide rises and the tide falls
I should have thought about that

and married myself a good lake sailor
whose boat goes out—and comes in—on the tide

江南曲

　　　　　李益

嫁得瞿塘賈，
朝朝誤妾期。
早知潮有信，
嫁與弄潮兒。

the poet mounted the high wall of the town
named "accepting surrenders" and heard
a flute playing

       —li yi

the sand spreads like a snowfield
before the watch tower in huile county

beyond the town named "accepting surrenders"
the moonlight is a blanket of frost

the soft melody of the flute
where is it coming from

all night the soldiers at their posts
look into the darkness for their homes

初上受降城聞笛

李益

回樂烽前沙似雪，
受降城外月如霜。
不知何處吹蘆管，
一夜征人盡望鄉。

late spring

    —han yu

meadows and trees know
that spring will be over soon

they vie with each other
with all the purples and reds
and fragrances of colors

poplars burst in white cotton
the elms follow
whirling white seeds in the air

what wisdom do they have
or talent
blowing around us like snow

晚春

    韓愈

草樹知春不久歸，
百般紅紫斗芳菲。
楊花榆莢無才思，
惟解漫天作雪飛。

wuyi lane

>   —liu yuxi

the weeds are in flower
beside the zhuque bridge

the evening sun drops low
at the entrance of wuyi lane

aristocrats wang and xie
lived here in jin dynasty

swallows nested in their houses
now ordinary people live with the birds

烏衣巷

劉禹錫

朱雀橋邊野草花，
烏衣巷口夕陽斜。
舊時王謝堂前燕，
飛入尋常百姓家。

song of the bamboo branch

—liu yuxi

No. 6

out in front of the town's western gate
the great rock stands in the middle of the river

powerful waves bash it year in and year out
but they cannot wash it away

it makes me sad the human heart
doesn't rest as solid as this stone

the heart goes to the east for awhile
and then goes west a split second later

竹枝詞（之六）

劉禹錫

城西門前灧澦堆，
年年波浪不能摧。
懊惱人心不如石，
少時東去復西來。

song of the bamboo branch

      —liu yuxi

No. 7

the jutang gorge has twelve rapids
the river rushes the channel
with a long swish and a roar

people have said since the old days
it's a hard way to go whatever you do

what a sorry business this is
how pitiful the human heart is

the rapids make wild waves in the gorges
but the trouble you make is shameful
when things run as smooth as open water

竹枝詞（之七）

劉禹錫

瞿塘嘈嘈十二灘，
人言道路古來難。
長恨人心不如水，
等閑平地起波瀾。

asking liu the nineteenth

—bai juyi

that newly made rice wine
not clarified of the rice yet
it is called the green ants wine

the little stove is made of red clay

it is going to snow
later in the afternoon

shall we get together
and have us a cup of the wine

問劉十九

白居易

綠蟻新醅酒，
紅泥小火爐。
晚來天欲雪，
能飲一杯無？

40

on the hardships of farmers

      —li shen

No. 1

they sow one seed of millet in spring
and harvest ten thousand in the fall
they do not waste an inch of ground anywhere
but they are still dying of famine

憫農（之一）

李紳

春種一粒粟，
秋收萬顆子。
四海無閑田，
農夫猶餓死。

41

on the hardships of farmers

       —li shen

No. 2

when they chop weeds at noon
the sun scorches their heads

they soak the ground underneath the rows
with the trickle of their sweat

count each grain in your dish
it grew from hard work and exhaustion

how many people know this

憫農 (之二)

　　　　　李紳

鋤禾日當午，
汗滴禾下土。
誰知盤中餐，
粒粒皆辛苦。

snow on the river

—liu zongyuan

no singing of birds in the mountain ranges
no footprints of men on a thousand trails
there is only one boat on the water
with an old man in a straw rain cape
who stands on deck and fishes by himself
where the snow falls on the cold river

江雪

柳宗元

千山鳥飛絕，
萬徑人踪滅。
孤舟蓑笠翁，
獨釣寒江雪。

hearing that le tian has been designated
the minister of war in jiangzhou

    —yuan zhen

the candle is guttering out
there is very little flame
I see shadows all around me

this evening I hear that my friend
has been demoted to jiujiang

even though I am sick to dying
I sit up in fear and surprise

this dark night the wind
blows a cold rain
through the cracks in my window

聞樂天授江州司馬
　　　元稹

殘燈無焰影幢幢，
此夕聞君謫九江。
垂死病中驚坐起，
暗風吹雨入寒窗。

44

huaqing palace

    —du mu

looking back again from changan
I see the beautiful palace

it stands like piles of silk
embroidered in the mountains

doors open one after the other
leading to the upper chamber

the plunging horse will soon
gallop into the palace yard

and yang the concubine is smiling
she is the emperor's favorite

she watches the clouds of red dust
you want to bet the litchi is coming

過華清宮絕句(之一)
杜牧

長安回望綉成堆，
山頂千門次第開。
一騎紅塵妃子笑，
無人知是荔枝來。

chibi

—du mu

the shattered halberd in the sand
is not totally corroded

I wash it and give it a polish
and it tells me of earlier dynasties

how general zhou in wu kingdom
had a lucky east wind

or else his wife and his lord's wife
the qiao sisters would have been caught by cao

he would have made them comfort him
locked in the bronze bird roof tower of wei

赤壁

杜牧

折戟沉沙鐵未消，
自將磨洗認前朝。
東風不與周郎便，
銅雀春深鎖二喬。

trip to the mountains

      —du mu

the narrow stone trail
winds far up into the mountains

this is a cloudy place
the cabins are almost invisible

I love seeing the maples at sunset
and pause in my cart to watch them

the leaves are as red
as prairies in the flowering spring

山行

杜牧

遠上寒山石徑斜，
白雲生處有人家。
停車坐愛楓林晚，
霜月紅于二月花。

anchored in qinhuai river

    —du mu

fog is shrouding the cold water
moonlight floods the sandy beach
my boat is anchored in qinhuai river
a wineshop is handy on the shore

the girl who entertains the patrons
she doesn't weep because the dynasty fell
she sings "flowers in the rear garden"
the lord who wrote the song lost the empire

泊秦淮

杜牧

烟籠寒水月籠沙，
夜泊秦淮近酒家。
商女不知亡國恨，
隔江猶唱後庭花。

short poem about spring south of the yangtze

—du mu

orioles are singing in a green and red
profusion of color for a thousand miles

in small towns along streams or on mountainsides
the wind blows the outdoor banners of the wine shops

they built four hundred and eighty monasteries
during the time of the southern dynasty

those buildings and their terraces
lie half hidden in the mist and the rain

江南春絕句

杜牧

千里鶯啼綠映紅，
水村山郭酒旗風。
南朝四百八十寺，
多少樓台烟雨中。

evening in august

      —du mu

red candles are burning
autumn is in the air
people are cold
and the room panels are cold

she swipes at fireflies with a little fan
a fan delicate and made of silk

she is sitting by the staircase
at the front of the house
the autumn wind
chilly as a mountain stream

she watches the one star and the other
altair and vega
the cowherd and the woman at the loom
from the old story

秋夕

杜牧

紅燭秋光冷畫屏，
輕羅小扇撲流螢。
天階夜色涼如水，
坐看牽牛織女星。

the scholar jia

—li shangyin

the emperor sought for talented officials
among the exiled ministers of han dynasty
he met with them at his wiyang palace

and jia the scholar came
no one could match his intelligence

the emperor spoke with him until midnight
they were so intense
leaning forward in the lotus position

the emperor wanted to know
 all he knew about ghost stories and the gods

jia could have told him how to save the state
take care of the ordinary people

賈生

李商隱

宣室求賢訪逐臣，
賈生才調更無倫。
可憐夜半虛前席，
不問蒼生問鬼神。

51

writing a letter to the north on a rainy night

　　　　—li shangyin

you ask me when I will be coming home
but I cannot tell you exactly

tonight the autumn rain on ba mountain
makes the ponds rise to overflowing

when will we be able to sit together
at the window that looks out on the west

just the two of us talking there so long
we will have to trim the wicks of our candles

speaking about our lives this night
when it was raining on ba mountain

夜雨寄北

　　　　李商隱

君問歸期未有期，
巴山夜雨漲秋池。
何當共剪西窗燭，
却話巴山夜雨時。

moon in late autumn when there is frost

     —li shangyin

as soon as we heard the calling of the geese
heading south in their high formations
we knew that the noise of the cicada was ended

on top of the pavilion a hundred feet up
you can see the water merge with the sky
far in the distance at the edge of things

the goddess of frost and snow deep in the heavens;
and chang er the woman who went to the moon
neither one of them is afraid of the cold

they cheer each other on to make the world lovely
the one covers the earth with a gleaming blanket
the other suffuses the darkness with her light

霜月

李商隱

初聞征雁已無蟬，
百尺樓高水接天。
青女素娥俱耐冷，
月中霜裏斗嬋娟。

an overlook for sightseeing

      —li shangyin

feeling sorrowful at the day's end
I drive my cart to the ancient overlook

the sun going down is truly beautiful
how sad the night comes so quickly after

樂遊原

      李商隱

向晚意不適，
驅車登古原。
夕陽無限好，
只是近黃昏。

memories in the riverside pavilion

　　　—zhao gu

as I climb the steps of the pavilion
my sadness confuses my heart

the moonlight on the water reflects the sky
who can tell the one from the other

those who enjoyed this light with me last year
where can I find them or turn to them now

and yet this still seems to be the same
moon-shadowed world we looked at then

江樓感舊

　　　　趙嘏

獨上江樓思渺然，
月光如水水如天。
同來望月人何處？
風景依稀似去年。

snow

　　　—luo yin

everybody says snow in winter
means a bumper crop next fall

what good did it do the last time
we had so much snow

there are a lot of poor people
living in changan city

we may need snow for a good harvest
but spare them the cruel blizzards

雪

　　　　　羅隱

盡道豐年瑞，
豐年事若何？
長安有貧者，
為瑞不宜多！

taicheng

—wei zhuang

heavy rains along the river
the grass on the banks is flourishing

six dynasties rose and fell here like a dream
now it is just the birds and their empty songs

willows drift in the winds of taicheng
like clouds of undulant smoke

they cover the ten-mile levee
as imperturbable as ever

台城

韋莊

江雨霏霏江草齊，
六朝如夢鳥空啼。
無情最是台城柳，
依舊烟籠十里堤。

a painting of jinling

—wei zhuang

who says when you are unhappy
you cannot finish a good painting

the painter feels
what everybody feels

please observe these six paintings
that reflect the southern dynasty

gnarled trees and cold clouds
see how they shadow the ancient city

金陵圖

韋莊

誰謂傷心畫不成？
畫人心逐世人情。
君看六幅南朝事，
古木寒雲滿故城。

peasant family

—nie yizhong

father cultivates the fields on the valley floor
his son tends the land at the foot of the mountain
their crops have not flowered yet in june
the state begins repairing the granaries

田家

聶夷中

父耕原上田，
子劚山下荒。
六月禾未秀，
官家已修倉！

passing through hucheng again

      —du xunhe

I stopped at the capital last year
and everybody was complaining

now this year I see
the administrator wearing a new red stole

he has smeared his badge of office
with the blood of the common people

再經胡城縣

      杜荀鶴

去歲曾經到縣城，
縣民無口不冤聲。
今來縣宰加朱紱，
便是生靈血染成。

on chrysanthemums

      —huang cao

they are in color everywhere in the courtyard
leaning against the chill of the west wind

no butterflies hang on the cold stamens
or linger in the pungent fragrance

if in some year I become the god of flowers
I will set them glowing among the peach blossoms

題菊花

黃巢

颯颯西風滿院栽，
蕊寒香冷蝶難來。
他年我若爲青帝，
報與桃花一處開。

chrysanthemums

  —huang cao

my chrysanthemums are flowering everywhere
in late autumn by the eighth of september
when five score other plants are withered

their sharp fragrance rises to the heavens
the whole city of changan is filled with it
my golden armor seizes every nook and cranny

菊花

黃巢

待到秋來九月八，
我花開後百花殺。
冲天香陣透長安，
滿城盡帶黃金甲。

mountain river with peach blossoms

      —zhang xu

far off the bridge seems to hover over the water
smoke from a hearth or meadow hangs in the trees

the water crashes over stone
the man signals the fisherman on the west side of the rock

peach blossoms those floating worlds of good fortune
drift on the river all day long

he knows of a cave but not where
he asks the fisherman on which side of the river

桃花溪

        張旭

隱隱飛橋隔野烟，
石磯西畔問漁船：
桃花盡日隨流水，
洞在清溪何處邊？

liangzhou song

—wang han

enticed by the rare grape wine in the wine glass
that polished cup so luminous in darkness
I would drink and drink again
but the thrummed strings in the pipa call me away
urging me again to horse and to war

do not mock me if I stretch out drunk or dead
on that battlefield where no life remains
how many ever survived to come home
since the old days in whatever the war

涼州詞

王翰

葡萄美酒夜光杯，
欲飲琵琶馬上催。
醉臥沙場君莫笑，
古來征戰幾人回？

border ballad

　　　—rong yu

the hu horsemen came raiding
they burned down many places in the mountains

the border town of suiye
that city's gate was not locked shut

guards on the watch towers
shouted from one to the other
all the way into the city

they knew the general was galloping
back from the night hunt

塞上曲

　　　　戎昱

胡風略地燒連山，
碎葉孤城未下關。
山頭烽子聲聲叫，
知是將軍夜獵還。

poem written for the south village of jun town

     —cui hu

last year on this morning
I walked through the village

in one courtyard
I saw the face of a woman
and the peach blossoms

a pale red reflecting pale red

now I see the courtyard empty
the woman no longer there

only the peach blossoms
tremble on the wind

題郡城南莊

    崔護

去年今日此門中，
人面桃花相映紅。
人面不知何處去，
桃花依舊笑春風。

the day before the qingming festival
when only cold food is served

—han xiong

blossoms were falling everywhere
in the city that spring
and the east wind rustled the willow
in the emperor's garden
on the day before qingming festival
commemorated the dead

at sundown that day in han dynasty
burning candles were handed out
so that cut willow branches
could be set on fire

and these were reserved
for the five noble eunuchs
honored with the title of hou
who incensed their courtyards and palaces
with the gray willow smoke

寒食

韓翃

春城無處不飛花，
寒食東風御柳斜。
日暮漢宮傳蠟燭，
輕烟散入五侯家。

67

anchored at night near maple bridge

—zhang ji

the old moon is going down
and the crows make a ruckus
the world is covered with frost

there are maples on the riverbank
and the lights of fishing boats
drift with the current

I fall into a sad sleep

the monastary on cold mountain
it is outside the town of gusu
the sound of its bell
touches the guestboat at midnight

楓橋夜泊

張繼

月落烏啼霜滿天，
江楓漁火對愁眠。
姑蘇城外寒山寺，
夜半鐘聲到客船。

looking for the recluse, but not finding him

—jia dao

I ask the boy under the pine trees

he says my master went off
to pick some medicinal herbs

he is a little way up on this mountain
but the clouds are so thick

I can't tell you where he is

尋隱者不遇

賈島

松下問童子，
言師採藥去。
只在此山中，
雲深不知處。

trip to lung xi

  —cheng tao

they swore they would wipe out the hu invaders
they didn't care about their own safety

five thousand lances were broken
when the hu horsemen struck them

it is so pitiful seeing the white bones
scattered along the river

these relics are the husbands of dreams
their wives are still waiting in their bedrooms

隴西行

    陳陶

誓掃匈奴不顧身，
五千貂錦喪胡塵。
可憐無定河邊骨，
猶是春閨夢裏人。

mice in the state granaries

—cao ye

mice in the state granaries are as big as buckets
they don't even run when you open the doors

soldiers at the front want food
ordinary people have to go hungry

who gave these big mice permission
to stuff their bellies all day long

官倉鼠

曹鄴

官倉老鼠大如斗，
見人開倉亦不走。
健兒無糧百姓飢，
誰遣朝朝入君口。

frustration in spring

—jin changxu

get rid of those pesky songbirds
they are as bad as my brothers noisy in the trees
they spoiled my sweet dream
just when I met my husband in liaoxi

春怨

金昌緒

打起黃鶯兒，
莫教枝上啼。
啼時驚妾夢，
不得到遼西。

suit woven of gold thread

> —du qiuniang

friend take my advice
don't worry about a gold-threaded suit

listen to me my friend
make the best of your spring days

go for the best of the flowers
when everything is in bloom

don't wait until the blossoms have fallen
what good will a branch do you then

金縷衣

杜秋娘

勸君莫惜金縷衣，
勸君惜取少年時。
花開堪折直須折，
莫待花無空折枝。